Psalms *for the* Heart

Presented to:

_____

Presented by:

_____

Date:

_____

Psalms
for the
Heart

God's Gift
of Inspiration,
Celebration, and Joy

Honor Books
Tulsa, Oklahoma

Psalms for the Heart
ISBN 1-56292-624-1
Copyright © 2002 by GRQ Ink, Inc.
1948 Green Hills Blvd.
Franklin, Tennessee 37067

Published by Honor Books
P.O. Box 55388
Tulsa, Oklahoma 74155

Developed by GRQ Ink, Inc.
Manuscript written by Angela J. Kiesling
Cover and text design by Whisner Design Group
Composition by Educational Publishing Concepts, Inc.

*May He grant you according
to your heart's desire,
And fulfill all your purpose.*

PSALM 20:4 NKJV

A Steadfast Heart

My heart is steadfast, O God;
I will sing and make music with all my soul.
Awake, harp and lyre!
I will awaken the dawn.
PSALMS 108:1-2 NIV

*E*arly morning is a lovely time of day, a time before daily

responsibilities demand our attention. Standing on a porch, eyes lifted to the trees, one can easily see why the psalmist chose to "awaken the dawn." Life is stirring all around, and song is filling the air—birds singing! Do they know instinctively that a Creator put music in their throats? Do they sing to Him?

Even when our own voice is silent, God hears the music of a happy soul, a soul that is steadfast in Him.

In that place of contentment, God's grace carries us along, preparing us for whatever the day may bring.

The birds nest beside the streams
and sing among the branches of the trees.
You send rain on the mountains
from your heavenly home,
and you fill the earth
with the fruit of your labor.
PSALMS 104:12-13 NLT

The Beauty of Change

The day is thine, the night also is thine:
thou hast prepared the light and the sun.
Thou hast set all the borders of the earth:
thou hast made summer and winter.

PSALMS 74:16-17

*A*lmost everyone loves summer, but winter's graces sometimes are not seen at first glance. Skeletal trees dot the landscape, and thin

grass clings to the hard-packed earth. Yet even in the stark lines of winter, we can see the work of a skillful Artist—One who knows that beauty is never static, that it is dependent on change.

The seasons are perhaps nature's best example of this. We watch as summer's bright greens give way to fall's warmer palette, then fade into winter's gray and white. Just when we long for the sight of green again, spring comes, bringing once more the buds of change and new life. God must have known we would need visuals to remind us of His purpose in change.

*L*ike the seasons, we are constantly changing—and growing richer
because of it. These nuances add color and beauty to our lives.

*I*n ages past you laid the foundation of the earth,
and the heavens are the work of your hands.
Even they will perish, but you remain forever;
they will wear out like old clothing.
You will change them like a garment,
and they will fade away.
But you are always the same;
your years never end.

PSALMS 102:25-27 NLT

Stoking the Heart-Fire

I lift up my eyes to you,
to you whose throne is in heaven.
PSALM 123:1 NIV

*B*uiding a fire is filled with anticipation. We choose something easily flammable as a starter and then position each piece of wood in an orderly pattern. We experience a thrill when oxygen feeds the fire and the fuel catches, and we lean back in satisfaction.

Sitting by a fire on a cold night is one of life's simple pleasures. We poke at the embers and watch, fascinated, as the sparks fly upward into the flue and disappear from sight. Just as we can stoke embers into a flame, God gives us constant reminders of himself—a momentary thought, the kindness of a stranger, a smile on a child's face—that stir our heart-fire into a warm, healthy glow. Then, like the sparks that are drawn upward, our thoughts rush to Him.

*G*od showers us with glimpses of grace. We thank God for His
nearness even when we least expect it.

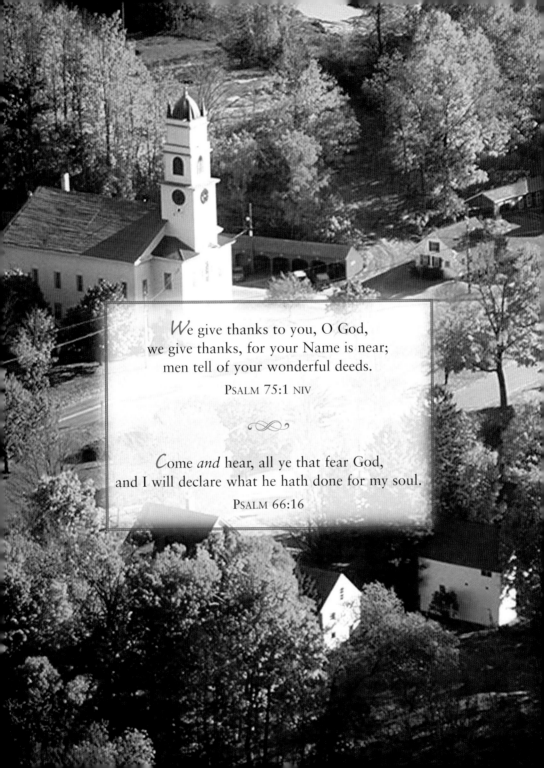

We give thanks to you, O God,
we give thanks, for your Name is near;
men tell of your wonderful deeds.

PSALM 75:1 NIV

Come *and* hear, all ye that fear God,
and I will declare what he hath done for my soul.

PSALM 66:16

A Childlike Heart

O Lord, my heart is not lifted up,
my eyes are not raised too high;
I do not occupy myself with things
too great and too marvelous for me.
But I have calmed and quieted my soul,
like a weaned child with its mother;
my soul is like the weaned child that is with me.

Psalms 131:1-2 NRSV

Small children have the ability to go with the moment, seizing whatever little joys they happen upon. Nothing is too small for their

wonder: a dandelion, a pile of crisp leaves, or an unexplored bit of terrain.

Watching children romp, we're reminded that play is their "work." Play is a time for unleashing imagination and creative energy. The heart of a child seems to embody all that God finds best about humankind. Maybe that's why David likened himself to a "weaned child," gladly deferring thoughts of things "too marvelous" for him to his Father. What greater image of contentment is there than that of a young child resting with complete trust on the shoulder of the one who loves him best?

Reveling in the moment brings out the child in us; it dispels worries
and sparks a sense of wonder for even the smallest details of life.

You had my mother give birth to me.
You made me trust you
while I was just a baby.
I have leaned on you since the day I was born;
you have been my God since my mother gave me birth.

PSALMS 22:9-10 NCV

The Heart of Forgiveness

HOW blessed is he whose transgression is forgiven,
Whose sin is covered!

The telephone rings, breaking the silence and bringing with it an unexpected gift: the forgiveness of a friend. A friendship is restored. Within seconds, joy replaces the heavy heart that weighed on us like an overstuffed backpack.

Nothing breathes new life into our souls like forgiveness, whether we receive it or give it to another. Amazingly, three small words take on a transforming power the moment they are uttered: *I forgive you*. How blessed we are when we hear these words! Forgiveness wraps us in a contentment that reaches deep into our heart. The most surprising gift of forgiveness is that it triggers a reciprocal response. In the moment we receive forgiveness, we are stirred to "do unto others" the very same thing.

If the gift of another's forgiveness can change us, imagine what
God's forgiveness can do!

*F*orget that I sowed wild oats;
Mark me with your sign of love.
Plan only the best for me, GOD!

PSALM 25:7 THE MESSAGE

A Trusting Heart

*Blessed is the man
who makes the LORD his trust,
who does not look to the proud,
to those who turn aside to false gods.*

PSALM 40:4 NIV

*L*earning to swim is daunting. Who can forget how it felt to squint across the pool before filling the lungs with that last deep

breath? Three strokes later, hesitant paddling ended in frantic sputtering when water started closing over the head. At the same moment that terror was about to strike, strong arms caught us from beneath and lifted us back up to the surface. Dad or Mom had been there all along.

A heart of trust is one of life's sweet but hard-won gifts. The discovery that God is always there, ready to lift us up when we start to sink, replaces fear with courage and timidity with boldness. Along with that courage and boldness comes the strength to face whatever life throws at us—even when it requires a long, scary swim to the other side.

*M*aking the decision to trust sometimes takes a leap of faith, but we
need not fear when God calls us to trust Him.

*I*n You, O Lᴏʀᴅ, I put my trust;
Let me never be ashamed;
Deliver me in Your righteousness.

Pꜱᴀʟᴍ 31:1 ɴᴋᴊᴠ

*T*rust in the Lᴏʀᴅ, and do good;
so you will live in the land, and enjoy security.

Pꜱᴀʟᴍ 37:3 ɴʀꜱᴠ

No Fear!

When the line of clothing called No Fear seized the youth market in the mid-1990s, bumper stickers sporting the logo appeared

on cars all across the nation. For the uninitiated, the words seemed puzzling. No fear? Why not? The designer's slogan was an appeal to its street-savvy customers, who would understand that the slogan represented a gutsy, no-holds-barred approach to a life lived to the extreme.

God preempted the popular slogan by several thousand years. He's always been in the no-fear business, giving us comfort in the midst of our darkest hours and guiding us back to the right path when we lose our footing. No amount of bravado can measure up to the heart that has learned the true meaning of having no fear.

When fear threatens to overtake us, we can turn to the One who fashioned us and knows us inside out. With God, there's always a path leading to higher ground.

*B*lessed be the Lord—
day after day he carries us along.
He's our Savior, our God, oh yes!
He's God-for-us, he's God-who-saves-us.
Lord GOD knows all
death's ins and outs.

PSALMS 68:19-20 THE MESSAGE

Answered Prayer Warms the Heart

In the day when I cried thou answeredst me,
and strengthenedst me with strength in my soul.
PSALM 138:3

*I*n the not-too-distant past, parents often summoned children for supper by means of a dinner bell. No matter where the children

played, the sound of Mama's bell brought them scrambling toward home. Through the years, the pattern remained the same: Mama called, and the children responded by showing up at the table. It was a summons, not just to eat, but to come *home*.

Now we are the ones who often do the calling, and we wonder: Does God hear us? Will He answer our prayers? We can have confidence in the fact that God not only hears but is faithful to answer our cries for help. Knowing that God is always ready to respond when we call to Him gives us boldness and strength. In Him we find our true home.

The fact that God bids us to call Him Father is a reminder that He considers us family. Like any good parent, He hears our requests—and answers them.

Hear a just cause, O LORD;
attend to my cry;
give ear to my prayer from
lips free of deceit.

PSALM 17:1 NRSV

An Eternal Perspective

You will keep on guiding me all my life with your wisdom and counsel; and afterwards receive me into the glories of heaven!
PSALM 73:24 TLB

⬥

*H*igh up in the Rockies, downhill skiing is treacherous if a skier diverts from the trail onto unmarked terrain. For this reason,

 occasional signs are posted to warn extreme skiers not to venture beyond the marked zones. Skiers who don't heed the signs risk their lives for a thrill-ride that may cross pits or rocks hidden by blankets of snow.

Signposts, warning lights, directional guides—all were created for one purpose: our safety. God, too, designed a system to ensure our safety. He promises to guide us through the labyrinth of life, offering His wisdom and divine counsel. Like the skiers, we have the choice to follow those guidelines. When we heed God's wisdom, His big picture unfolds before us.

⬥

When we follow God's path, He keeps us safe from harm and leads us, step by step, to our intended destiny.

*F*rom now on every road you travel
Will take you to GOD.
Follow the Covenant signs;
Read the charted directions.

PSALM 25:10 THE MESSAGE

God Satisfies the Soul

For He satisfies the longing soul,
And fills the hungry soul with goodness.
PSALM 107:9 NKJV

*H*olidays and special occasions are universally celebrated by feasting. Sharing food around a table bonds people together, and

"Pass the peas, please" branches into meaningful conversation. The sharing of food leads to the sharing of words and the sharing of hearts.

In the same way, we can continually feast on the goodness of God, which satisfies our soul-hunger like nothing else can. Out of that fullness comes a desire to feed others with the blessings God has showered on us. When we give out of our abundance, we are filled even more. Our plate is never empty; our souls are always full.

*W*henever we share a meal with friends and loved ones, we remember the greater food that God gives, the food that fills our hungry soul to overflowing.

The LORD is my strength and my shield;
in him my heart trusts;
so I am helped, and my heart exults,
and with my song I give thanks to him.

PSALM 28:7 NRSV

Finding Favor with God

Keep me as the apple of the eye,
hide me under the shadow of thy wings.
PSALM 17:8

As parents, we try never to have favorites among our children. With the birth of each child comes a love tailor-made just for him or her. David unabashedly assumed he was the apple of God's eye—a favored son. From that place of special favor, he asked for the Lord's protection. In intimate language, he depicted a mother hen covering her hatchlings—whenever startled, the chicks run toward their mother, and she lifts a protective wing to hide them.

Does God play favorites? God makes each one of us his favorite. He lifts a spreading wing to cover us with warmth and safety. Being a favored son or daughter entitles us to the bounty of God's goodness and grace, which endures forever.

When we realize just how special we are to God, it gives us the courage to seek His face, not just His hand.

Restore us, O Lord God Almighty;
make your face shine upon us,
that we may be saved.

Psalm 80:19 niv

The Heart of Courage

Be strong, and let your heart take courage,
all you who wait for the LORD.
PSALM 31:24 NRSV

*W*hat does it really mean to "wait for the Lord"? If we're honest, most of us don't like waiting. Waiting means deferring our wants and needs—sometimes to the point of despair. Another version translates this verse "all you who *hope* in the Lord." *Hope* is expectation, and it hints at more to come. It's easier to hope than to wait.

Our human nature craves quick replies and speedy results, but God has a different timetable, one that seems to tick more slowly than our own. Perhaps that is why all who hope in the Lord are encouraged to be strong and courageous. Those who wait for God are rewarded with a satisfied heart—a heart of courage.

*O*ur heart grows strong as it waits for the Lord, who rewards those
who trust in Him.

It is good for me to draw near to God:
I have put my trust in the Lord GOD,
that I may declare all thy works.

PSALM 73:28

The Shepherd's Heart

THE LORD is *my shepherd;*
I shall not want.
He maketh me to lie down in green pastures:
he leadeth me beside the still waters.
PSALMS 23:1-2

*S*heep respond to a voice—especially the voice of their shepherd. Amazingly, some shepherds claim to know the sound of an individual

sheep's bleat, even when the sheep calls out from the midst of a large herd. One shepherd named each of her sheep and recognized their voices when they called to her. She attests to the fact that sheep are known also for their instinct to follow. They will

follow her wherever she leads, whether high up on a rocky slope, down into a grassy pasture, or back to the paddock for shearing time.

The twenty-third psalm depicts a Good Shepherd who leads us to safety and nourishes the soul. We know that we are safe with the Good Shepherd and that He is keeping watch on the horizon.

*W*hen God leads, do we always follow? Though often headstrong,
we inevitably find that the path is easier when we allow Him to point
the way.

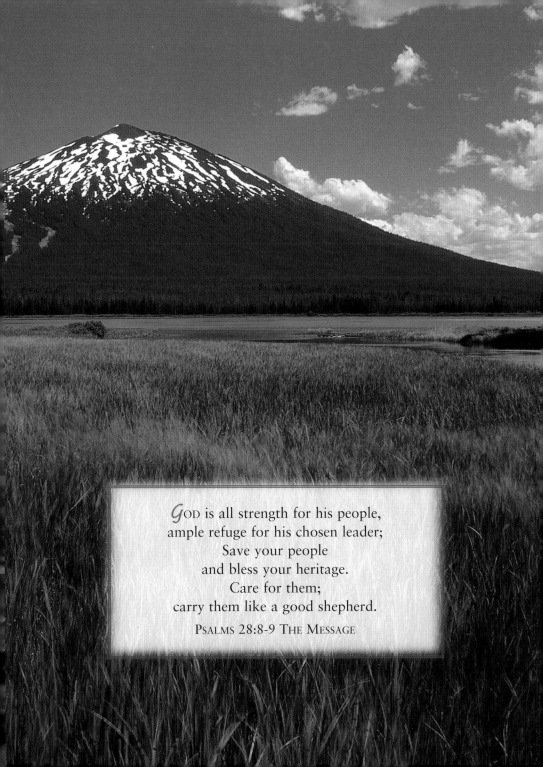

GOD is all strength for his people,
ample refuge for his chosen leader;
Save your people
and bless your heritage.
Care for them;
carry them like a good shepherd.

PSALMS 28:8-9 THE MESSAGE

Rest for the Weary Heart

Oh that I had wings like a dove!
for then *would I fly away,*
and be at rest.

PSALM 55:6

Most of us have experienced the sensation of flying in a dream—and reveled in it. *To be like the birds,* we think, *and just fly away when the world presses in too closely.* We long to have "wings like a dove," but most of the time we feel more like chickens, flapping miserably around in the barnyard, unable to get off the ground for sustained flight.

When we are bone-weary and eager to fly away, God promises to give us rest and sustain us. In that place of physical—and spiritual—exhaustion, a divine paradox emerges: When we are weak, He becomes strong *in us.* Our very weakness is a tool that magnifies His glory.

God never promised we wouldn't grow weary in this life. He only promised that He would lift us up when we call out to Him. Hard times become a showcase for His strength, which is made perfect in weakness.

O my God, my soul is in despair within me;
Therefore I remember You from the land of the Jordan
And the peaks of Hermon, from Mount Mizar.

PSALM 42:6 NASB

A Heart on High

BLESS the LORD, O my soul;
And all that is within me, bless *His holy name!*
PSALM 103:1 NKJV

Certain overlooks along the Blue Ridge Parkway demand attention the way a harvest moon draws eyes to the night sky. The scenic route twists and winds for more than four hundred miles along the crests of the Blue Ridge and Smoky Mountain ranges, offering views of stunning peaks and spectacular valleys wrapped in the hazy blue mist that earned the mountains their name. We stop, and our breath catches suddenly in our throat. Our perspective changes as we look out, and our worry diminishes. God's awesome creation lifts our heart.

The mountaintop panorama inspires us to praise God. Paradoxically, when we praise Him, we are blessed in return. Our heart soars.

Giving ourself over entirely to God's praise makes us recipients of His incredible grace.

*H*allelujah!
It's a good thing to sing praise to our God;
praise is beautiful, praise is fitting.

PSALM 147:1 THE MESSAGE

Thirsting for God

*A white-tailed deer drinks
from the creek;
I want to drink God,
deep draughts of God.*
PSALM 42:1 THE MESSAGE

*S*oft drinks, sweetened iced tea, and flavored sparkling water
rank high on today's list of preferred beverages. When we're parched
from heat or exercise, however, the only thing
we want is pure water. The psalmist used the
metaphor of a deer panting for water to
describe his thirst for God. A deer slaking its
thirst will sink its muzzle into a stream long
enough to satisfy its craving.

When we thirst deep in our soul, we, like the deer, instinctively
turn to the Source that refreshes. God fills our need and sustains us for
the task at hand. We drink—and are fortified by Him.

*J*ust as He created our bodies to hunger and thirst, God put a deep
longing for Himself within us—a yearning that is satisfied only by
turning to Him.

He makes springs pour water into the ravines;
it flows between the mountains.
They give water to all the beasts of the field;
the wild donkeys quench their thirst.

PSALMS 104:10-11 NIV

The Blessedness of Helping

BLESSED is *he that considereth the poor:*
the LORD *will deliver him in time of trouble.*
PSALM 41:1

*S*tepping out of the convenience store, we spot him—again. The

same man who perched against the
window ledge a week ago, flashing a
little card asking for money. Over at
the Kmart, a Salvation Army worker
clangs her handbell rhythmically,
scanning the holiday shoppers as they
rush past and hoping to meet a pair
of friendly eyes.

Giving brings out the best in us and makes us a little bit more like
God, the greatest Giver of all. And when we go through our lives with
a perpetual attitude of giving, we are prompted to help when we're
least aware of our helpfulness.

*W*hen we give to others—of our time, resources, and friendship—we
are blessed beyond measure. God always sees to it that our cup
overflows when we stop to fill another's cup first.

*T*hey give generously to those in need.
Their good deeds will never be forgotten.
They will have influence and honor.

PSALM 112:9 NLT

A Pure Heart

God's words are pure words,
Pure silver words refined seven times
In the fires of his word-kiln.
PSALM 12:6 THE MESSAGE

⌒∞⌒

*O*nce a ceramist creates a figure, the object must be baked under extreme heat before it's ready for use. The firing process delays the

enjoyment of the object, and yet if the ceramist skips this process, the object will be useless. The beauty and service of the piece are strengthened for having "passed through the fire."

God must refine us, too, through the fires of adversity. Sometimes that refining process takes the shape of waiting; other times that process allows us to suffer losses, great or small. The process may be as mundane as finding contentment in our ordinary lives, or it may be as intense as facing a life-threatening illness. In the end, we are rendered more beautiful and useful to God by having passed through the fire.

⌒∞⌒

When God turns up the heat on our life, He purifies our motives and
clarifies our vision. What can seem like the lifting of His favor may
actually be a blessing in disguise.

Happy are those who live pure lives,
who follow the LORD's teachings.
Happy are those who keep his rules,
who try to obey him with their whole heart.

PSALMS 119:1-2 NCV

Hope's Reward

*O*n the heels of World War II, Peter Marshall, the celebrated United States Senate chaplain during the 1940s, offered a famous

prayer called "Bifocals of Faith." Before the statesmen of his day, he prayed, "God, give us the faith to believe in the ultimate triumph of righteousness, no matter how dark and uncertain are the skies of today. We pray for the bifocals of faith—that see the despair and the need of the hour but also see, further on, the patience of our God working out His plan in the world He has made."

Hope springs from a heart that trusts in God. Without hope, our lives would quickly turn bleak. But with this virtue in our hearts, every dark and uncertain sky holds clouds with silver linings.

God can open our eyes to see through the lens of faith, so that our heart may rest in the peace that comes from trusting Him.

I find rest in God;
only he gives me hope.
He is my rock and my salvation.
He is my defender;
I will not be defeated.

PSALMS 62:5-6 NCV

Delight in His Will

I delight to do Your will, O my God,
And Your law is within my heart.

PSALM 40:8 NKJV

Most of us mark the arrival of a new year through the simple task of hanging a fresh calendar on the wall. Flipping through it, we

may pause to scan the pages of the months ahead and wonder what they hold in store for us. Will March bring a surprise blessing? Will there be a disappointment in September? What will happen between now and when December rolls around again?

Though we anticipate the future, and sometimes worry about it, God is the One who sets our course and imprints each day with the events that become our life. A heart committed to the Lord can leave the calendar in His hands and trust that He will fill in the blanks with perfect order.

Even when circumstances don't go our way, we delight to do God's will. In His perfect timing, the right path emerges, and our heart is lifted up.

Great are the works of the LORD,
studied by all who delight in them.
Full of honor and majesty is his work,
and his righteousness endures forever.

PSALMS 111:2-3 NRSV

Reaping a Joyful Heart

Sing for joy to God, our strength;
shout out loud to the God of Jacob.
PSALM 81:1 NCV

A trip to the beach on a hot summer day is a ticket to leisure for most folks. Strolling along the shore, one can watch surfers bobbing

like corks as they wait for the next big breaker. Giant waves that would scare most swimmers produce a thrill for good surfers, who glide along the waves rather than get pounded by them. In the same way, author Jim Reimann observed that "the things we try to avoid and fight against . . . are the very things that produce abundant joy in us."

True joy, it has been said, is not built on passing things; rather, true joy is built on the unchangeable love of God. Whether the events we face are ordinary or terrifying, they are powerless to separate us from God's love.

No momentary thrill can compare to the deep, abiding joy that seeps into our heart every time we remember that God calls us His own.

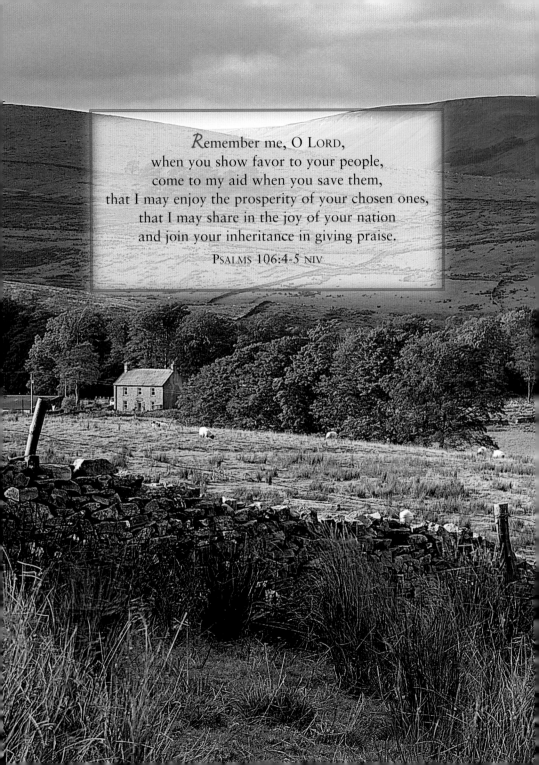

*R*emember me, O L<small>ORD</small>,
when you show favor to your people,
come to my aid when you save them,
that I may enjoy the prosperity of your chosen ones,
that I may share in the joy of your nation
and join your inheritance in giving praise.

P<small>SALMS</small> 106:4-5 <small>NIV</small>

The Meditative Heart

I will meditate in thy precepts, and have respect unto thy ways. I will delight myself in thy statutes: I will not forget thy word.

PSALMS 119:15-16

*T*he word *library* calls to mind a specific image: a large room with floor-to-ceiling shelves, tables with people sitting hunched over

their books, and nothing but the sound of rustling pages—the sound of studying. There's something consoling about a quiet time of study.

When the words we meditate on come from God, we are fortified in our spirit as well as our mind. A heart that is soaked in the knowledge of God changes from the inside out. If we continue to meditate, we will discover that what started as a discipline has turned to a delight.

*S*teeping ourselves in the words of life paves the way for God's blessing. As we meditate, He unfolds His perfect plan for our lives.

You made me willing to listen and obey.
And so, I said, "I am here to do what is written about me
in the book, where it says,
'I enjoy pleasing you. Your Law is in my heart.'"

PSALMS 40:6-8 CEV

The Divine Gatekeeper

The Lord is thy keeper:
the Lord is thy shade upon thy right hand.
Psalm 121:5

*T*hroughout history, gatekeepers filled a crucial role. From their lookout, they could see who was approaching the city and determine  whether that person—or group of people— should be allowed inside the city walls. They kept out and ushered in as they saw fit, all with the best interests of the city's inhabitants in mind.

How sure our step becomes when we know the Lord is our gatekeeper—the One who allows us to come and go in safety, the One who causes us to pass through where we might not have passed otherwise. It's comforting to know that this same gatekeeper also bars our entry to any place that might bring us harm. He knows when to open doors and when to close them. With God as our Keeper, we never have to fear where our foot falls.

*T*he knowledge that God is going before us, keeping us as no one else can, gives us peace.

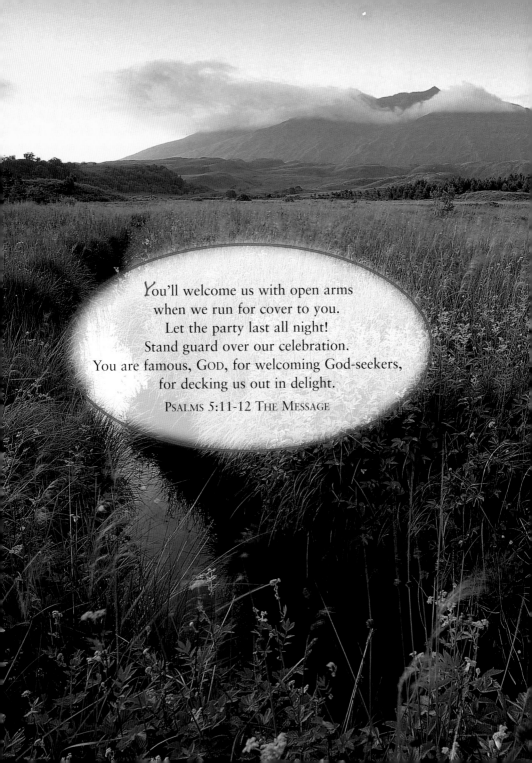

You'll welcome us with open arms
when we run for cover to you.
Let the party last all night!
Stand guard over our celebration.
You are famous, GOD, for welcoming God-seekers,
for decking us out in delight.

PSALMS 5:11-12 THE MESSAGE

Healing the Broken Heart

A rare, blooming bush takes a long time to cultivate. Even when its buds finally open up and hold their blossoms to the sun, these

blooms can be crushed in an instant. Yet, over time, the heart of the bush can be restored, and it can once again sprout new blossoms, sometimes even more beautiful than the first. With tender care, the stalks grow strong again, capable of sending roots deep into the earth where it can find lasting nourishment.

When and how God chooses to comfort us may come as a surprise, but comfort almost always arrives in the form of another human being. The right words, spoken at the right time, lift our broken heart—our broken spirit—and give us hope that life will go on.

God's grace pours out upon us, healing the broken places in our heart
and restoring a sense of purpose to our life.

*S*ing to the LORD, all you godly ones!
Praise his holy name.
His anger lasts for a moment,
but his favor lasts a lifetime!
Weeping may go on all night,
but joy comes with the morning.

PSALMS 30:4-5 NLT

The Waiting Heart

TRULY my soul silently waits for God;
From Him comes my salvation.
PSALM 62:1 NKJV

⌒∞⌒

*N*o amount of worrying can make things happen, let alone make them happen the way we want. Still, our human nature, bent on trying, rises to the challenge. What's the remedy for this all-too-common malady? Oswald Chambers, in his classic *My Utmost for His Highest*, wrote, "When God brings a time of waiting, and appears to be unresponsive, don't fill it with busyness, just wait. . . . If you have the slightest doubt, then He is not guiding."

The story of Abraham and Sarah illustrates the futility of trying to make a divine promise come about in our own timing. Tired of waiting for a son, Sarah took matters into her own hands. The result was disastrous. God's timetable always delivers an Isaac rather than an Ishmael.

⌒∞⌒

The adage "Good things come to those who wait" can't be found in Scripture, but God seems to prove its truth again and again. He showers us with blessings when we wait for his perfect timing.

I WAITED PATIENTLY for God to help me; then he listened and heard my cry. He lifted me out of the pit of despair, out from the bog and the mire, and set my feet on a hard, firm path and steadied me as I walked along.

PSALMS 40:1-2 TLB

Praise in the Evening

*Oh, bless the L*ORD*, all you servants of the L*ORD*,*
you who serve as night watchmen
*in the house of the L*ORD*.*
PSALM 134:1 NLT

*T*he night sky, stitched with a pattern of glittering stars, hangs
like a dark quilt over the landscape when viewed in the country.
Without competition from city lights, the stars
appear brighter and much more numerous.
Shooting stars dart toward earth every now
and then, and we wonder why we missed
out for so long on this cosmic slide show.

If the cosmos could sing, the galaxies would rise
up to praise their Maker. Nighttime rituals, whether of stars or human
beings, mark the end of the day and set the stage for reverence. Like
the night watchmen who guarded Israel's temple, we are drawn to
quiet praise and thankfulness for all God's goodness. And even when
words fail us, a silent praise speaks for us deep within our hearts.

God's majesty calls forth a sense of wonder in us. In awe of His
mighty works, we let our soul well up with praise for Him.

*P*RAISE ye the LORD:
for *it is* good to sing praises
unto our God.

PSALM 147:1

The Amazing Grace of God

Who is like the LORD our God,
who is seated on high,
who looks far down
on the heavens and the earth?
He raises the poor from the dust,
and lifts the needy from the ash heap,
to make them sit with princes,
with the princes of his people.

PSALMS 113:5-8 NRSV

*L*ike a father who stoops to pick up his child when she skins her knee, God is constantly on the lookout, ready to rescue His beloved—

us. Scripture says that He bends down from Heaven to deal in the affairs of humankind, lifting us up when we're on the ash heap of life. He not only lifts us from the dirt, He sets us in places of healing and favor, where our heart is strengthened and our spirit renewed.

Though we may not always be aware of it, God's grace is poured out on our lives day after day. It marks our steps and directs our course. Because of His goodness, we can never escape His notice—not even if we try.

God gives us glimpses of His grace in the everyday events of our life.
His compassion hems us in on all sides.

*G*od All-Powerful, come back.
Look down from heaven and see.
Take care of us, your vine.
You planted this shoot with your own hands
and strengthened this child.

PSALMS 80:14-15 NCV

Traveling Mercies

When a person's steps follow the LORD,
God is pleased with his ways.
If he stumbles, he will not fall,
because the LORD *holds his hand.*

PSALMS 37:23-24 NCV

$\mathcal{G}$uide horses on group trail rides are seldom picked for their beauty. Instead, the rancher chooses horses that are surefooted. The

 horses we find most beautiful are known for their refined breeding and high spirits. But the plodding, surefooted breeds have a high reputation of dependability on the trail or in a harness. Their work ethic is unmatched.

Life's journey is fraught with unexpected twists and turns, and the risk of stumbling ranks high on the list of road hazards. No doubt the psalmist knew this, but he had the boldness to pen words that comfort us centuries later: When God holds us by the hand, a stumble doesn't result in a fall. With His supporting arm, we catch our footing and continue surefooted along the trail.

$\mathcal{G}$od plants our feet firmly on the path and rejoices in every step we take that follows His leading. His traveling mercies will cover us all the days of our life.

*T*urn to me and have mercy on me,
as you always do to those who love your name.
Direct my footsteps according to your word;
let no sin rule over me.

PSALMS 119:132-133 NIV

Growing Wiser

*Thou through thy commandments has made me
wiser than mine enemies: for they are ever with me.
I have more understanding than all my teachers:
for thy testimonies are my meditation.*

PSALMS 119:98-99

*T*he passing down of wisdom from parent to child, like links in
an ancestral chain, gives character a chance to take root in new soil. If

watered, nourished, and pruned regularly, a
seedling will grow into a beautiful tree—broad,
tall, and capable of casting a long shadow. It
will give back to its environment and provide
shade to those who gather its acorns. So, too,
does a child mature and become an adult.

Wisdom shows up best, not in the things we
choose, but in the things we don't choose. With
God as our Gardener, we flourish in the place where He plants us,
enriching even those outside our borders.

*G*odly wisdom is a lasting heritage—a priceless treasure that we are
privileged to pass on to our descendants. With wisdom guiding our
heart, we will not stray too far from the right path.

A good person speaks with wisdom,
and he says what is fair.
The teachings of his God are in his heart,
so he does not fail to keep them.

PSALMS 37:30-31 NCV

The Feasting Heart

You serve me a six-course dinner
right in front of my enemies.
You revive my drooping head;
my cup brims with blessing.

PSALM 23:5 THE MESSAGE

*F*ood gives us the energy to keep going. There's no sign more welcome at the end of a long day on the road than RESTAURANT.

Turning in, we anticipate the satisfying meal that waits inside. Once filled, we are revived and fortified for the next leg of our journey.

In the same way, God allows us to fill up from time spent with Him. If our day is hurried and stressed, we may only have time for brief snacks—and even then He stokes our spiritual energy. But once we settle in for a full-course spiritual meal, we realize what we've been missing and eat heartily.

When our soul hungers for more of God, He is more than ready to meet our spiritual need. Our emptiness is an open invitation for His divine nourishment.

My soul longs, indeed it faints
for the courts of the LORD;
my heart and my flesh sing for joy
to the living God.

PSALM 84:2 NRSV

Refuge for the Heart

Incline your ear to me;
rescue me speedily.
Be a rock of refuge for me,
a strong fortress to save me.

PSALM 31:2 NRSV

*L*ighthouses are pictures of steadfastness. Battered by hurricane-force gales, pelted by sea spray, and baked by the sun, those stone giants cling year after year to the coastline. They stand sometimes for centuries, and they fascinate us. A favorite with artists and photographers, lighthouses come to mind when we think of words like *refuge, strong,* or *fortress,* words that were used to describe God when David penned the thirty-first psalm.

Lighthouses not only stand against the elements and offer a stark beauty to the seascape, but they also literally save lives. They guide ships to safety by throwing light out into the night, beckoning the captains to shore. In a similar way, we might easily stray into dangerous waters if not for God's light thrown on our path.

God is immovable, even in the midst of our very transient troubles.
He delights to rescue His children, displaying His strength for the
whole world to see.

My honor and salvation come from God.
He is my mighty rock and my protection.
People, trust God all the time.
Tell him all your problems,
because God is our protection.

PSALMS 62:7-8 NCV

A Humble Heart

*B*ack in the days when mothers sewed their children's clothes, dressmaking was a big event, especially when the dresses were cut

from cloth that had been set aside for Easter. A girl would watch eagerly as her mother's fingers transformed the fabric into a dress with the girl's very own dimensions.

Sometimes the excitement faded when a girl realized her sisters' dresses were not only going to be made from the same cloth, but they would be made from the same pattern as well. Then the mother would add a little touch that made each dress distinct—a lace collar, a scalloped edge, or a looping rickrack design. Though simple, the dresses were masterpieces—distinct and beautiful for each girl.

*H*umility clothes us in beauty and becomes a stamp of individuality. When we set our heart on God, He makes us more like Him.

The LORD is King forever and ever;
Nations have perished from His land.
O LORD, You have heard the desire
of the humble;
You will strengthen their heart,
You will incline Your ear.

PSALMS 10:16-17 NASB

Hidden in the Secret Place

Thou art *my hiding place;*
thou shalt preserve me from trouble;
thou shalt compass me about
with songs of deliverance.
PSALM 32:7

A secret childhood hiding place can be so vivid in our memory
that at times it flashes back in Technicolor. Perhaps our hiding place

was the broad branch of a tree where
we could perch unseen thanks to the
cover of a thousand green leaves. Or
perhaps it was a shallow cave cut into
the side of a slope or a small glade
hidden behind a willow tree that formed
a leafy curtain. We felt safe in our secret

place—wonderfully alone, yet not fearful.

Years later, God still hides us in the secret place of His protection.
Though God's secret place is not tangible with leafy borders, our spirit
recognizes at once how real this wonderful hiding place is. And we are
at peace.

Even when circumstances confound us, God hides us in the safety
of His embrace. Like David, we find peace in knowing He is
always there.

*R*escue me from my enemies, O LORD,
for I hide myself in you.
Teach me to do your will,
for you are my God;
may your good Spirit
lead me on level ground.

PSALMS 143:9-10 NIV

Nature: God's Herald

Thou crownest the year with thy goodness; and thy paths drop fatness. They drop upon *the pastures of the wilderness: and the little hills rejoice on every side. The pastures are clothed with flocks; the valleys also are covered over with corn; they shout for joy, they also sing.*

PSALMS 65:11-13

Young schoolchildren often take nature walks with brown paper bags in hand. As they set out on the trail, a teacher instructs them to

bring back as many intriguing bits of nature as they can find: an acorn, a brightly colored leaf, a pine needle, a flower bud, an empty cocoon.

As adults we may not venture outdoors with a bag in hand, but like children we can stop and marvel at God's fingerprint on the world around us. We see it everywhere we look in nature, from the intricacy of a flower stamen to the watercolor brilliance of a sunset. Apart from the glory of nature, we also see God's artistic expression in His crowning achievement in creation: each other.

Sometimes God speaks loudest—and most eloquently—through nature. In every detail of creation we see His handiwork, reminding us that He's interested in the details of our lives too.

*H*e covers the heavens with clouds, sends down the showers and makes the green grass grow in mountain pastures. He feeds the wild animals and the young ravens cry to him for food.

PSALMS 147:8-9 TLB

Joy of the Bridegroom

The sun comes out like a bridegroom from his bedroom.
It rejoices like an athlete eager to run a race.
PSALM 19:5 NCV

*T*his verse paints a word-picture of a new day bursting forth into the world with the joy and vigor of a bridegroom fresh from his wedding chamber. In the brightness, we sense God pouring out on us an unquenchable love.

Each new day bears God's stamp of approval that He sees in His creation. Each new day is delivered to us like a wrapped package that contains the gift of life. The very air we breathe bears witness to His overwhelming kindness toward us. Every sunrise reminds us of the unique opportunity to praise Him. There will never be another day just like today.

*N*o matter how we feel at any given moment, we can rest in the knowledge that God swoons with love for us, like a bridegroom for his beloved. He is a faithful Husband who promises never to leave or forsake us.

Make glad the soul of Your servant,
For to You, O Lord, I lift up my soul.
For You, Lord, are good, and ready to forgive,
And abundant in lovingkindness
to all who call upon You.

PSALMS 86:4-5 NASB

The Blessings of Long Life

The righteous flourish like the palm tree,
and grow like a cedar in Lebanon.
They are planted in the house of the LORD;
they flourish in the courts of our God.
In old age they still produce fruit;
they are always green and full of sap.

PSALMS 92:12-14 NRSV

*O*ccasionally we spot an elderly couple who still hold hands and gaze into each other's eyes like newlyweds. *What's their secret?* we wonder. If we investigate a little more deeply, we'll usually find two people who are lifelong examples of the second greatest commandment: Love your neighbor [or spouse] as yourself. Time has etched deep lines on their faces and stooped their bodies, and yet their spirits remain sound and supple— and as full of life as when they first caught sight of each other and recognized a kindred spirit.

Although we long for fairy-tale romances that require no effort, we often find that the quintessential ingredient to every good relationship is, after all, a servant's heart.

*T*he choice to love that we make today will bear fruit for many years
to come, and we will reap the fruit of that love in old age. Let us not
squander the precious gift of time.

*H*e will call upon me, and I will answer him;
I will be with him in trouble,
I will deliver him and honor him.
With long life will I satisfy him
and show him my salvation.

PSALMS 91:15-16 NIV

The Singing Heart

O sing to the LORD a new song,
For He has done wonderful things,
His right hand and His holy arm have gained the victory for Him.
PSALM 98:1 NASB

*T*he giant oak tree outside the bedroom window was home to a vocal mockingbird. In the silver darkness just before dawn, the bird would throat up, mimicking the songs of other birds and singing a full repertoire of tunes. And when the mockingbird had whistled its way through every last one, it would start all over again like a CD stuck on continuous play. At first the repetitive singing was obnoxious, and then, considered from another perspective, humorous. In the end, listeners thought that it was a rare treat to wake to the sound of singing so vibrant that it stirred all nearby to life.

Who but God could stir the mockingbird to such a songfest, day in and day out?

Regardless of our mood today, we choose to align ourself with the psalmist in praise of our Maker. God's daily goodness is reason enough for rejoicing.

*H*ALLELUJAH! YES, LET his people praise him as they stand in his Temple courts. Praise the Lord because he is so good; sing to his wonderful name.

PSALMS 135:1-3 TLB

Sweeter than Honey

How sweet are Your words to my taste,
Sweeter than honey to my mouth!
PSALM 119:103 NKJV

*C*urling up with a good novel on a quiet day is one of life's underrated pleasures. We open the pages, and the world around us fades away while we're drawn, willingly, into the story before us. The author's words weave their magic, changing us if only slightly.

Who can deny the power of words to inspire, to deflate, to encourage, to discourage, to help, to hurt? The psalmist found the words of God not bittersweet, as so much human-inspired language turns out to be, but "sweeter than honey." Unlike our own words, His words are always life-giving. Though we may find pleasure in other books, the one God wrote has the power to transform us from the inside out. No wonder this perennial bestseller has stood the test of time.

Like the hymnist, we rejoice to know "the wonderful words of life." They not only move us, they change us—little by little—into the image of the Author.

I will sing unto the LORD as long as I live: I will sing praise to my God while I have my being. My meditation of him shall be sweet: I will be glad in the LORD.

PSALMS 104:33-34

Heart in a Hurry

Wait and trust the LORD.
Don't be upset when others get rich
or when someone else's plans succeed.
PSALM 37:7 NCV

*W*hy is it easier to grieve with those who grieve than to rejoice with those who rejoice? When someone else's dream comes true, we

may feel genuine happiness for our friend, but deep inside a small voice cries out, *Lord, have you forgotten about me?* We thank Him for the good that He has brought into the lives of others but wait anxiously for the day when it will be *our* turn.

One Bible version records it this way: "Be still before the Lord and wait patiently for him" (NIV). God is never in a hurry, but so often we are. All things happen, not in *due* time, but in *divine* time. There's no need to hurry, after all. God has everything under control and right on schedule, in divine time.

When our hearts are in a hurry, we need to stop and remember that our timetable is not the right one. The Lord will renew us as we wait on Him and on His perfect plan.

*O*ur soul waits for the LORD;
he is our help and shield.
Our heart is glad in him,
because we trust in his holy name.
Let your steadfast love, O LORD, be upon us,
even as we hope in you.

PSALMS 33:20-22 NRSV

The Message in the Gates

Lift up your heads, O ye gates;
and be ye lift up, ye everlasting doors;
and the King of glory shall come in.

PSALM 24:7

*G*ates frame the walled city of Jerusalem. The gates still retain a noble look, thousands of years after their construction. Though most of us will pass through thousands of gates and doors in our lifetime, we rarely stop to think about what they signify. Gates and doorways are intriguing. They are entry as well as exit points. They allow people and objects to come in and go out. They protect and defend. They include and exclude.

Do we open our hearts to others? When we let people enter the doorway to our hearts, what do they find? Do they sense welcome and peace? Do they know instinctively that God's Spirit dwells there?

Let us try to make our hearts a place where peace resides. Let all who pass through the gate of our lives be inspired to lift up their heads.

*O*pen for me the gates of righteousness;
I will enter and give thanks to the LORD.
This is the gate of the LORD
through which the righteous may enter.

PSALMS 118:19-20 NIV

Lord of the Night

If I say, "Surely the darkness shall cover me,
and the light around me become night,"
even the darkness is not dark to you;
the night is as bright as the day,
for darkness is as light to you.
PSALMS 139:11-12 NRSV

*W*aking up in the wee hours of the night, we find that all is still and black as pitch. As we walk to the refrigerator for a drink, our eye is drawn to peek outside at the night sky, the backyard, and the woods that fringe the edge of the lawn. What is it about nighttime that calls the spirit toward fear or peace?

When he penned the lines of Psalm 139, David prefaced them with these rhetorical questions: Where could I go from Your Spirit? Or where could I flee from Your presence? David knew that even the darkness cannot hide us from God's watchful eyes and blanketing care. The darkness need not hold fear for us. And that is reason enough to find peace in the night.

God's protective covering stills us in the darkness of night and revives us by the light of day. No matter where we turn, there He is— already—before us.

By day the LORD directs his love,
at night his song is with me—
a prayer to the God of my life.

PSALM 42:8 NIV

Lord of the Light

I BLESS THE Lord: O Lord my God, how great you are! You are robed
with honor and with majesty and light! You stretched out the starry
curtain of the heavens.

PSALMS 104:1-2 TLB

*H*ow reviving light is! After the long stretch of night, the sun's
morning rays are a welcome sight, pushing through the trees and

making dappled patterns on the ground. In a
very real sense, our body responds to
sunlight. Sunlight helps set our biological
clock, lift our mood and immune system,
and even produce vitamin D to keep us
strong and well.

Scripture reminds us that God is "robed with majesty and light."
The One who burst onto the scene of early creation with light—the
sun by day, the moon and stars by night—fills us with another, more
stirring kind of light when we spend time with Him. The light of God
fills us with His goodness.

*T*oday is a gift of divine love and light. We embrace each moment,
reveling in the knowledge that it was created for us.

If I rise with the sun in the east
and settle in the west beyond the sea,
even there you would guide me.
With your right hand you would hold me.

Psalms 139:9-10 NCV

Staying Young at Heart

Who satisfies your mouth with good things,
So that your youth is renewed like the eagle's.
PSALM 103:5 NKJV

❦

*W*ho hasn't felt the downward drag of fatigue, whether induced by age, stress, or a bout of illness? When our body lacks vigor, we

 long for—and remember—the feeling of vitality more than ever. And in these times we recall that God promised to renew our youth like the eagle's.

When we watch an eagle fly, we can see how effortlessly it seems to navigate the sky. Though equipped with wings that can reach ninety inches wide, this powerful bird glides for long distances on columns of rising air called thermals. In the same way, God carries us on the strength of His wings, giving us spiritual, emotional, and physical vitality when we most need it. As we ride His divine thermals, we remember once again how we thrive in His care.

❦

The circumstances of life may seem to crowd around us, but in
God's strength we can rise above them and soar with renewed vigor.

From the ends of the earth I call to you,
I call as my heart grows faint;
lead me to the rock that is higher than I.
For you have been my refuge,
a strong tower against the foe.

PSALMS 61:2-3 NIV

Tears in a Bottle

Thou tellest my wanderings:
put thou my tears into thy bottle:
are they not in thy book?
PSALM 56:8

*T*his verse paints a word-picture that is both hard to believe and awe-inspiring at the same time. Like a woman who saves a rare

perfume in a bottle, God stores our tears in His bottle and records them in His book. The divine Keeper chronicles every twist and turn we take down the path of life.

When David wrote this psalm, he was running for his life from King Saul's men. His cry to the Lord did not fall on deaf ears; his tears were not wasted. Neither are ours. Though we may not be in mortal danger, it's a comfort to know that God notes our every teardrop, just as He sees when one tiny sparrow falls from a tree.

God is a Friend to the sorrowful and calls us blessed when we mourn,
for we will in due time be comforted. And with the comfort we
receive, we are equipped to soothe others when sorrow strikes them.

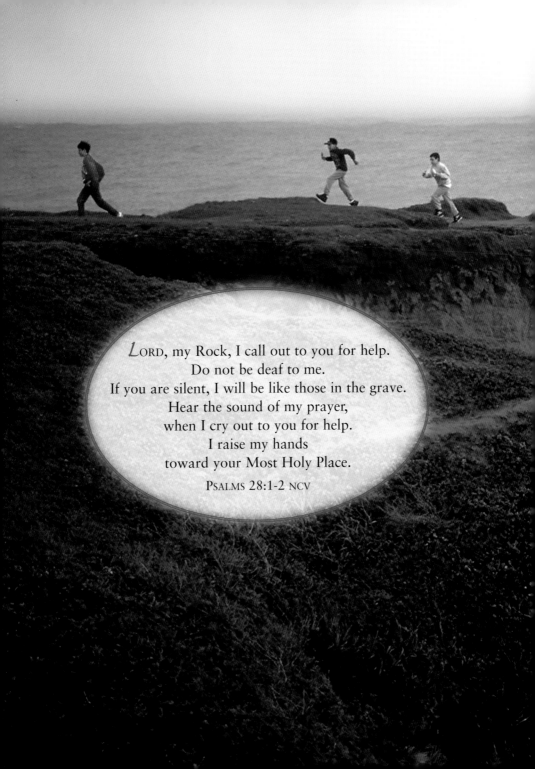

LORD, my Rock, I call out to you for help.
Do not be deaf to me.
If you are silent, I will be like those in the grave.
Hear the sound of my prayer,
when I cry out to you for help.
I raise my hands
toward your Most Holy Place.

PSALMS 28:1-2 NCV

A Heart of Remembrance

Come and hear, all you who fear God,
and I will tell what he has done for me.
PSALM 66:16 NRSV

*N*o doubt, the art of storytelling dates back to the Garden of Eden, and for good reason. We all enjoy the pleasure factor of a good

story. Even more, however, we enjoy the purpose—and the memories—that we find in stories. Through oral histories we learn what went before us, and through them we pass on what has happened in our own lives so that time will not erase our experiences.

Erecting personal memorials of our life—stories, photo albums, family traditions, prayer journals, and the like—commemorates the blessings that come our way. When we "tell of what He has done," we are twice blessed: in seeing the joy it brings to others and in the reliving of our story.

*W*e remember the good things God has done in our life and pass them on so that others can be blessed too.

GIVE thanks to the LORD, for He is good;
For His lovingkindness is everlasting.
Give thanks to the God of gods,
For His lovingkindness is everlasting.

PSALMS 136:1-2 NASB

God's Awesome Deeds

You faithfully answer our prayers with awesome deeds,
O God our savior.
You are the hope of everyone on earth,
even those who sail on distant seas.

PSALM 65:5 NLT

*A*ncient seamen thought that if they sailed too far and skirted too close to the horizon they would fall off the edge of the earth.

Sometimes our life feels much the same way. We struggle to navigate through choppy waters and imagine the worst. But when we call out to God for guidance, He surprises us with awesome deeds—answers to prayer that surpass our understanding.

No matter what happens today, we know that our life is in the same hands that hold the earth steady on its axis. God is faithful to act, to answer prayers, and to perform His amazing feats—all in His perfect timing.

God's intervention in our life is nothing short of awesome. We rejoice in His perfect will and perfect timing for the events of our life.

*I*n you our ancestors trusted;
they trusted, and you delivered them.
To you they cried, and were saved;
in you they trusted, and were not put to shame.

PSALMS 22:4-5 NRSV

God's Words Restore the Heart

Your word, O LORD, is eternal;
it stands firm in the heavens.
PSALM 119:89 NIV

*A*t the end of Mark Twain's classic *Tom Sawyer*, the boy-hero of Hannibal, Missouri, uncovers a treasure buried in the cavern that nearly claimed his life. The town rejoices at Tom's good fortune, and

we, the reader, get to peek over his shoulder, vicariously experiencing the thrill of finding something long buried and of great worth.

That's just the sort of word-picture that David painted in Psalm 119. Like a newly discovered treasure, God's words fill us with joy and the promise of lifelong provision, no matter how many times we read them. When we uncover this cache of riches, we become heir of a fortune that transcends earthly values. To our surprise, we find that for the first time in our life our cup runs over, just as the psalmist said it would.

We are filled with the treasure of God's life-giving words, that we may grow wise and full of Godly light. God's words restore our soul and bring hope to the hopeless.

Your goodness continues forever,
and your teachings are true.
I have had troubles and misery,
but I love your commands.
Your rules are always good.
Help me understand so I can live.

PSALMS 119:142-144 NCV

Joy in Lowly Tasks

A single day spent in your Temple is better than a thousand anywhere else! I would rather be a doorman of the Temple of my God than live in palaces of wickedness.

PSALM 84:10 TLB

*W*hether it's pausing to wipe peanut butter from a child's face or picking up stray bits of trash in a neighbor's yard, our little deeds

of kindness speak a love language all their own—the language of God's love. In these mundane tasks we find a simple kind of joy that comes from giving without strings attached. That joy is its own reward.

Translated to a modern setting, this psalm might celebrate the church sexton who vacuums the carpet every week, the altar guild member who polishes the brass communion plates, or the teenage boy who pulls weeds from the church's flower bed. Though these jobs carry little prestige, the faithful performance of them doesn't go unnoticed by God. When we work for Him, we are in the employment of the King.

*L*et God find a heart that is ready and willing to do His will, whatever that may be. No job is too small to glorify His name.

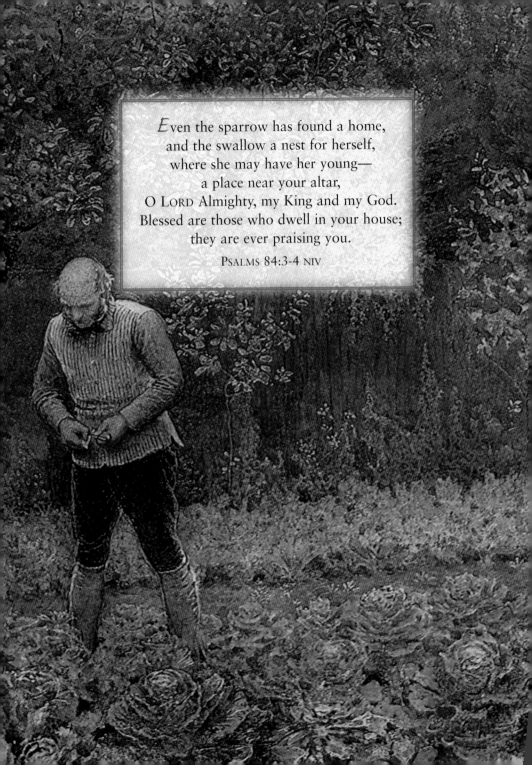

*E*ven the sparrow has found a home,
and the swallow a nest for herself,
where she may have her young—
a place near your altar,
O LORD Almighty, my King and my God.
Blessed are those who dwell in your house;
they are ever praising you.

PSALMS 84:3-4 NIV

The Teachable Heart

Teach me thy way, O LORD; I will walk in thy truth:
unite my heart to fear thy name.
PSALM 86:11

Saint Augustine once wrote to a young pupil, "Education is the food of youth, the delight of old age, the ornament of prosperity, the

refuge and comfort of adversity, and the provocation to grace in the soul." No matter how much traditional education we get, however, it can't compare with the sort of schooling that God gives.

It has been said that life is a classroom and that God is our constant Teacher. A teacher can only teach a willing pupil, however, so we must yield to God's authority. Through the patient repetition of life's lessons and a gentle and a not-so-gentle prodding, God proves to be a Schoolmaster who always transforms those who submit to His teaching. Like the psalmist, when we learn His way, we will walk in His truth.

Our heart is open to the Lord's gentle prodding. When we follow His
lead, wonderful treasures of learning open before us.

*T*he LORD has rewarded me according to my righteousness;
According to the cleanness of my hands He has recompensed me.
For I have kept the ways of the LORD,
And have not wickedly departed from my God.

PSALMS 18:20-21 NASB

God's Strength Is Enough

Powerful is your arm!
Strong is your hand!
Your right hand is lifted high in glorious strength.
Psalm 89:13 nlt

*T*o small children, we adults must look like giants. We tower over them and stoop a long way down to pick them up in our arms. In the instant we do, our intimidating strength blurs into a single gesture of tenderness. Sometimes that's how we see God—vast and mighty and towering in strength high above us. The moment He folds us in His arms, however, we remember that He is, after all, our Daddy.

When we grow weak and afraid, the image of God's strong arms brings a fresh reminder of His nearness. The Lord is quick to save His children when we call on Him, and He promises to keep us in the palm of His hand. There, safe in the grasp of the Almighty, we find the courage and strength to do whatever He asks of us.

*G*od delights to show His mighty power at work in our life. When we trust in His strength, amazing things happen.

With a strong hand, and with a stretched out arm: for his mercy *endureth* for ever. To him which divided the Red sea into parts: for his mercy *endureth* for ever.

PSALMS 136:12-13

A Searching Heart

The righteous *cry out, and the* LORD *heareth,*
and delivereth them out of all their troubles.
PSALM 34:17

⌘

Camping out deep in the woods, we notice that night falls quickly and thickly. The darkness wraps everything in its blanket of black, making a flashlight the camper's best friend in an emergency. The camper's watch snags on the foliage, snapping from his wrist, so he retraces his steps with the light beamed out in front of him, illuminating the ground. He hears rustling in the bushes and shines the flashlight in that direction, searching for the source.

In a similar way, our heart beams out into the darkness, calling to God when we're troubled or simply in need of an answer. He promises that when we search for Him, we will find Him. Often what we find is that His answer is already on the way.

⌘

Even before the answer comes, we know that God has heard our
prayer and is working to answer it in His way, in His time.

*R*ise up, be our help,
And redeem us for the sake of Your lovingkindness.

PSALM 44:26 NASB

God's Merciful Heart

As parents feel for their children,
GOD feels for those who fear him.
He knows us inside and out,
keeps in mind that we're made of mud.
PSALMS 103:13-14 THE MESSAGE

*K*ermit Roosevelt, the son of Teddy Roosevelt, once wrote, "The great man never loses his child's heart. What is true of the Kingdom of

God must also be true in the affairs of men." If a loving earthly father feels for his children, how much more is our Heavenly Father moved with compassion for us? This psalm captures God's tender thoughts toward us. Another version says, "He remembers that we are dust."

Can mud and dust ever have any hope of attaining Godlikeness? The question needs no answer because we know all too well our own shortcomings. The miracle of life, breathed into our body clay, opens the doorway to something even more miraculous, if we but reach out and take it: God's own life in us.

*G*od's mercy conceals our human frailties and forgives our every transgression. When we receive His mercy, we, in turn, long to give it away.

Comfort me with your love,
as you promised me, your servant.
Have mercy on me so that I may live.
I love your teachings.

PSALMS 119:76-77 NCV

A Bountiful Crop

They sowed fields and planted vineyards
that yielded a fruitful harvest;
he blessed them, and their numbers greatly increased,
and he did not let their herds diminish.

PSALM 107:37 NIV

*A*merican writer George Grant wrote a letter home to his wife about what he called "one of London's most delightful gardens"

nestled within the tiny churchyard of Saint Mary's parish. Most intriguing of all was a bronze plaque in one corner that declared A GOOD THEOLOGY WILL INVARIABLY PRODUCE A GOOD GARDEN.

Grant was at first amused by the epigram but later realized that the words conveyed what he called a scriptural world-view: a solid theology always takes into consideration the link between the profound and the mundane. Like tending a garden, Grant said that cultivating a balanced view of God involves "both the drudgery of daily labor and the high ideals of faith, hope, and love. But the results are always worth the extra effort."

By tending to both the daily routine and the high ideals of our life,
we reap a bountiful crop of God's goodness. Our faithfulness paves
the way for His blessing.

*E*very one of these depends on you to give them
daily food. You supply it, and they gather it.
You open wide your hand to feed them and they
are satisfied with all your bountiful provision.

PSALMS 104:27-28 TLB

A Time to Be Loud

Hallelujah!
I give thanks to GOD with everything I've got—
Wherever good people gather, and in the congregation.
PSALM 111:1 THE MESSAGE

⌒✕⌒

Sometimes our joy is so tangible we feel we might burst if we don't get it out. At those times, we may want to climb to the rooftop

and shout out the goodness of God. All creation praises Him, from the crickets' nighttime chorus to the wind's whistling through the eaves. And if we ceased to proclaim His goodness, Scripture says that the miraculous would take place: the rocks themselves would cry out. Imagine such a sight—a true rock concert of praise!

There's a time and place for quiet, meditative faith. There's a time and place for silent prayer. And there's a time and place for soft, worshipful singing. And there's a time and place to praise God with all the gusto we can muster. Yes, there is a time to be loud.

⌒✕⌒

God's presence fills us with joy unspeakable and begs for release. We will shout His praise as long as we live!

PRAISE the LORD!
Praise, O servants of the LORD.
Praise the name of the LORD.
Blessed be the name of the LORD
From this time forth and forever.

PSALMS 113:1-2 NASB

Along the Footpath

Make me go in the path of thy commandments;
for therein do I delight.

PSALM 119:35

*I*n his poem "The Road Not Taken," Robert Frost talks about two paths that diverge in a wood and how he chose the "one less traveled by." He culminated this poem with these words: "and that has made all the difference." Like the poet, we

may ponder what may have happened if we had veered down the road not taken, but ultimately, it's the road *taken* that molds us into the people we turn out to be—for better or for worse. How blessed we are when we choose the path that leads to God!

Just as a footpath through the woods winds its way past twisting roots and low-hanging branches, the narrow way that leads to God may be full of obstacles. Someday we'll be able to look back and rejoice over the road not taken.

*W*e *face choices today that may have lifelong results. With God's help, we can choose the way that leads to life—and Him.*

I will follow your rules forever,
because they make me happy.
I will try to do what you demand
forever, until the end.

PSALMS 119:111-112 NCV

A Lasting Heritage

The LORD *is the portion of mine inheritance and of my cup:*
thou maintainest my lot.
The lines are fallen unto me in pleasant places;
yea, I have a goodly heritage.

PSALMS 16:5-6

*T*he word *inheritance* denotes good things to come, a promise of unexpected blessings. We would be delighted to hear that a distant

relative had willed property or wealth to us. Just the knowledge that we had been chosen, handpicked to receive the blessing, would trigger a rush of feeling.

The psalmist rejoiced that the God who hung the stars in their places was his Inheritance, that the One who spoke the world into existence was his Portion. The same is true for us when we call God our Father. This is no distant relative, no remote kin who leaves us a fortune. Though God owns all the cattle on all the hills, as His heirs we claim riches of another kind—and the best gift is still to come, on the day when we will receive Him face to face.

*T*he legacies we leave, and receive, in this lifetime cannot compare
with our heritage as God's children.

*T*he LORD will not cast off his people, neither will he forsake his inheritance.

PSALM 94:14

Wholesome Preservatives

*L*ike the biblical Joseph, Patrick was sold into slavery as a teenager when marauding Irishmen raided the English coastal regions where he lived. During his years as a slave, this son of a deacon turned to God with a zeal that wouldn't let him go. After escaping to England, he dreamed that an Irishman begged him to return and preach to his countrymen. Patrick did return to Ireland as a missionary and became the Emerald Isle's most beloved saint—Saint Patrick.

We read much about the preservatives that go into our food, stripping them of their organic value. One kind of preservative, however, is good for our bodies as well as our souls: God. He protects us from evil and preserves our "going out" and "coming in." As Joseph and Patrick discovered, what comes disguised as evil, God often uses for good.

*G*od's protection surrounds us. No matter what happens, we know
He has our ultimate good at heart.

I WILL extol thee, O LORD; for thou hast lifted me up, and hast not made my foes to rejoice over me. O LORD my God, I cried unto thee, and thou hast healed me.

PSALMS 30:1-2

The Compassionate Heart

The Lord is gracious, and full of compassion;
slow to anger, and of great mercy.
Psalm 145:8

*T*he caterpillar doesn't argue that it would rather be a butterfly. It simply submits to the plan that God created for it and curls up inside the cocoon while the miracle takes place. When the transformation is complete, a different creature emerges from the cocoon and flies away to begin its new life with wings.

In His mercy, God transforms us as well—if we let Him. He exchanges our impatience for grace and our anger for compassion. After His work is complete in us, we emerge as someone better than we were before. With God's love and grace inside us, we, like Him, become slow to anger and quick to love.

*W*hen we act in love rather than anger, we extend God's gift of
compassion to others. Best of all, we find that with regular practice it
is easier to love.

*L*ORD, hear my prayer;
listen to my cry for mercy.
Answer me
because you are loyal and good.

PSALM 143:1 NCV

A Heart at Peace

I will lie down and sleep in peace,
*for you alone, O L*ord*,*
make me dwell in safety.
P*salm* 4:8 niv

❧

A good night's sleep is one of those small blessings that is often taken for granted until we lose it. Peaceful sleep? David could

appreciate it more than the average person. He was a man who slept in caves while on the run from a king with murderous intent. Yet even in the midst of life-threatening danger, his heart was at peace because he knew that God alone made him dwell in safety.

No dead bolt or bar at the window can replace the serenity that comes from trusting God for our security. Because of His night watch over us, we can crawl into bed and sleep the deep slumber of children, comforted by the knowledge that God is guarding us body and soul.

❧

We're never too old for this classic children's prayer: "Now I lay me down to sleep; I pray Thee, Lord, my soul to keep. Watch over me all through the night, and keep me safe till morning light."

*R*eturn to your rest, O my soul,
For the LORD has dealt bountifully with you.
For You have rescued my soul from death,
My eyes from tears,
My feet from stumbling.

PSALMS 116:7-8 NASB

Skillfully Wrought

*You made all the delicate, inner parts of my body
and knit me together in my mother's womb.
Thank you for making me so wonderfully complex!
Your workmanship is marvelous—and how well I know it.*

PSALMS 139:13-14 NLT

A mirror can be our best friend or our worst enemy. Like a funhouse mirror, we often carry a distorted image of ourself, forgetting

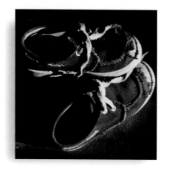

that the special quality that makes us *who we are* is found in no other human being on earth. Maybe it's the way we tilt our head when we talk, or the way we burst into laughter at unexpected moments. Perhaps others see a sparkle in our eyes that we never knew was there. Beyond the physical, we each possess qualities that make us a true original. God said so, and His workmanship is marvelous.

When we glimpse a newborn baby, we take note of his tiny fingernails, her very small eyebrows. Our loving Father crafted every detail of that baby.

When we see ourself through God's eyes, we behold a complex and wonderful work of art. He really did break the mold when He made us!

*H*e determines the number of the stars;
he gives to all of them their names.
Great is our Lᴏʀᴅ, and abundant in power;
his understanding is beyond measure.

Psᴀʟᴍs 147:4-5 ɴʀsᴠ